NS

5WP

WHY SHOULD I TURN DOWN THE VOLUME?

✦ and other questions about healthy

eyes and ears ✦

Louise Spilsbury

www.heinemann.co.uk/library

Visit our website to find out more information about **Heinemann Library** books.

To order:
☎ Phone 44 (0) 1865 888066
🖹 Send a fax to 44 (0) 1865 314091
💻 Visit the Heinemann Bookshop at www.heinemann.co.uk/library to browse our catalogue and order online.

First published in Great Britain by Heinemann Library, Halley Court, Jordan Hill, Oxford OX2 8EJ, part of Harcourt Education.
Heinemann is a registered trademark of Harcourt Education Ltd.

Editorial: Nancy Dickmann, Jennifer Tubbs and Louise Galpine
Design: David Poole and Tokay Interactive Ltd (www.tokay.co.uk)
Illustrations: Kamae Design Ltd
Picture Research: Rebecca Sodergren and Liz Eddison
Production: Séverine Ribierre and Jonathan Smith

Originated by Ambassador Litho Ltd
Printed in China by Wing King Tong

ISBN 0 431 11095 6
07 06 05 04 03
10 9 8 7 6 5 4 3 2 1

British Library Cataloguing in Publication Data
Spilsbury, Louise
Why Should I Turn Down the Volume? and other questions about healthy eyes and ears
612.8'4
A full catalogue record for this book is available from the British Library.

Acknowledgements
Corbis pp. **5** (LWA: Sharie Kennedy), **11** (Bob Mitchell), **12** (Rob Lewine), **13** (Eye Ubiquitous: Robert & Linda Mostyn), **15** (Jose Luis Pelaez), **26** (Laura Dwight); Getty Images pp. **4**, **14**, **21** (Imagebank), **23** (Stone), **8**, **20**, **22**, **27** (Taxi), **28**; Science Photo Library pp. **10**, **17**, **18**, **19**, **25**; Trevor Clifford p. **16**; Tudor Photography pp. **9**, **24**.

Cover photograph of child with earphones, reproduced with permission of Tudor Photography.

The publishers would like to thank Julie Johnson for her assistance in the preparation of this book.

Every effort has been made to contact copyright holders of any material reproduced in this book. Any omissions will be rectified in subsequent printings if notice is given to the publishers.

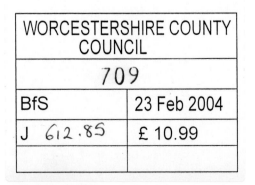

CONTENTS

Why should I take care of my eyes and ears?   4

How do eyes and ears work?   6

Why shouldn't I put things in my ears?   9

What should I do about earwax?   10

Why should I turn the volume down?   12

What is an ear infection?   14

Do I need to clean my eyes?   16

Why do my eyes get sore?   18

Why should I wear sunglasses?   20

Why do I have to take computer breaks?   23

Why should I use a reading light?   24

Why should I have my eyes and ears checked?   25

Eye and ear facts   29

Glossary   30

Further reading   31

Index   32

Words appearing in the text in bold, **like this**, are explained in the Glossary.

WHY SHOULD I TAKE CARE OF MY EYES AND EARS?

You have five **organs** of sense – eyes to see, ears to hear, a nose to smell, a tongue to taste and skin to feel. Together, your five senses give you all the information you need to live and learn. Your sight and hearing are probably the most important senses of all.

Your eyes tell you what things look like and where they are, from the tiniest grains of sand to the big screen. Your ears listen out for sounds as quiet as your cat purring to your friends shouting encouragement at a sports match. They also help you to keep your balance.

Your eyes and ears help you to enjoy the world around you, but also keep you safe. When you are out, your eyes enjoy the views and watch out for road signs. Your ears hear birdsong and listen out for traffic noises.

Delicate organs

You should take care of your eyes and ears because they are delicate organs that are easily damaged. They will only work well if you look after them properly. To keep them and the rest of your body healthy, you should eat a well-balanced diet with lots of fruit and vegetables, and get plenty of sleep.

HEALTHY TIPS

Here are some tips for looking after your eyes and ears.

- Never put or poke anything into your eyes and ears, or anyone else's.

- Do not throw sand, stones or dirt at other people, and do not let them throw these things at you.

- Never run while you are carrying scissors or other sharp objects.

The old saying that eating carrots helps you to see in the dark may not be exactly true, but fruit and vegetables do contain vitamin A, which keeps your eyes working well.

HOW DO EYES AND EARS WORK?

When you look at an object, the cornea, a clear cover at the front of the eye, helps the eye to focus on it. Light from the object enters the eye through the **pupil**, which is the black hole in the middle of the iris (the coloured part of the eye). Muscles in the iris make the pupil bigger or smaller to let more or less light in. Then the **lens** focuses the light onto the **retina**, a thin layer at the back of the eye.

The retina changes the light patterns that it receives into signals. These signals travel to the brain along the optic nerve. The brain changes the signals into a picture, so you can see what you are looking at. All this happens incredibly quickly.

When an image arrives at the retina, it is upside-down! The brain simply turns it the right way up.

eyeball

muscles

cornea

pupil

retina

optic nerve

lens

iris

How do ears hear?

Any sound makes the air vibrate (move backwards and forwards). These vibrations are called sound waves. The **outer ear** catches these sound waves and takes them into your **ear canal**. When sound waves hit the **eardrum** – a very thin skin stretched across the ear passage – they make it vibrate like a drum. The eardrum is joined to tiny bones called ossicles, so they vibrate, too.

The ossicles pass the sound waves to a coiled-up tube, called the **cochlea**. The cochlea is filled with fluid and tiny hairs. The sound waves move the tiny hairs. The movements set off nerve signals in the auditory (hearing) nerve, which goes to your brain. Your brain works out what the signals mean so that you can hear what is going on.

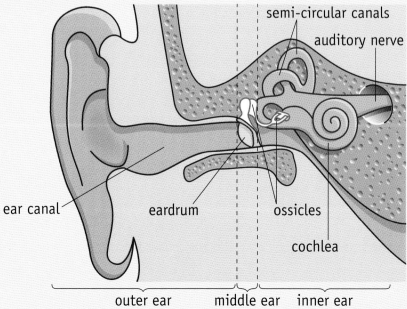

semi-circular canals

auditory nerve

ear canal

eardrum

ossicles

cochlea

outer ear   middle ear   inner ear

Your ears have three main parts – the outer ear, the **middle ear** and the **inner ear**. The semi-circular canals are filled with fluid and hairs, and they help you to keep your balance.

It is the fluid in their semi-circular canals that helps these children balance like this!

WHY DO I GET DIZZY?

If you whizz around on a roundabout for too long, the fluid in your semi-circular canals keeps moving for a few moments after you stop. This makes you feel dizzy.

How do ears help me to balance?

Your ears help you to balance by being aware of the smallest movement in your body. They do this using three bony tubes, called semi-circular canals, found above the **cochlea**. They contain fluid that moves when you do. The fluid also moves bendy stalks linked to nerve **cells** in the canals, and this sends signals to your brain. You have three different semi-circular canals, so your body can sense the three different types of movement – side-to-side, twisting and nodding.

WHY SHOULDN'T I PUT THINGS IN MY EARS?

An old saying goes, 'Never put anything in your ear that is smaller than your elbow'. Now, no one is suggesting that you would even want to put an elbow in your ear, but it helps you to remember that you should never put things inside your ear.

Use a clean, soapy flannel soaked in warm water to wipe around your **outer ear**. When you wash your hair, water will wash into your ears to clean them.

How can ears be hurt?

Some people stick cotton buds or other things inside their ears to clean them out or to scratch them. In fact, it is very dangerous to poke about inside your ears with anything. The skin of the **ear canal** and the **eardrum** is very thin and fragile. These delicate and important parts can be easily injured if they are poked and prodded.

9

WHAT SHOULD I DO ABOUT EARWAX?

Earwax may not look very nice sitting in your outer ear, but it has a very important job to do in protecting the delicate inner parts of your ear.

Earwax is the brown, shiny, sticky stuff you sometimes see in your ear. It is perfectly normal and healthy to have small amounts of earwax in your ear. You do not need to do anything special to get rid of it. Washing your ears regularly is enough to keep them clean.

What does earwax do?

Earwax is a defence against dirt and **germs**. It contains special chemicals, which kill germs that get inside the **ear canal**. This stops the germs from causing **infections**. Earwax also stops dirt, dust and any other tiny bits in the air from getting to your **eardrum**. Bits like these stick to the gummy earwax, and get washed out with it later on.

Where does earwax come from?

Special **glands** in the **outer ear** canal make earwax. The proper name for earwax is cerumen. After the glands make wax, it slowly moves through the outer ear canal towards the opening of the ear. Here, it dries up and tumbles out of the ear, or is wiped out of your ear when you wash it.

WHAT IF EARWAX BLOCKS MY EARS?

If you think that you have too much earwax in your ears or that earwax is blocking your ears, you should see a doctor. Sometimes, doctors give people ear drops, which help to break down the earwax and get rid of it. Remember, though, never to put medicine in your ears unless a doctor tells you to.

Earwax also coats the skin inside your ear with a waterproof layer. Water runs out of your ear, rather than hanging around to become a trap for germs.

WHY SHOULD I TURN THE VOLUME DOWN?

If someone else can hear the music coming through your headphones, then it is too loud and may be damaging your ears.

We hear sounds all the time – the television, radio, computer, traffic, people shouting in the playground and chattering in the classroom. Most of the time, our ears can cope with all this noise but, if sounds are too loud or go on for too long, your hearing can be damaged.

Loud sounds are bad

When you hear a sudden loud noise, such as fireworks, or listen to loud sounds for too long, say, at a concert, some of the tiny hairs in the **cochlea** can be destroyed. Unlike other parts of your body, such as your skin, these fragile hairs cannot repair themselves. You have about 60,000 of these hairs but, each time you lose a few, your hearing works a little less well.

What happens to your hearing?

Some people lose their hearing for a short time after listening to loud noise. Others may get tinnitus. Tinnitus is when you hear ringing, whistling or buzzing sounds inside your ear. These things usually pass quite quickly but, each time they happen, your hearing weakens a little. Do your best to avoid loud noises, and protect your ears with ear plugs when you cannot avoid them.

WHAT SOUNDS ARE TOO LOUD?

The loudness of a sound is measured in decibels. Sounds under 75 decibels should not hurt you, but listening to sounds over 90 decibels too closely for too long can damage your ears.

- Refrigerator humming: 40 decibels
- Normal conversation: 60 decibels
- City traffic: 80 decibels
- Front rows of rock concert: 110 decibels
- Military jet take-off: 140 decibels

People who work with noisy machinery wear earplugs or earphones to protect their ears.

13

WHAT IS AN EAR INFECTION?

Many children get ear **infections** – in fact, most have had at least one ear infection before they are two years old! An ear infection is when **germs** get inside your ear and cause you pain or make you ill.

Outer ear infections

Outer ear infections are also called 'swimmer's ear', because people who swim a lot often get them, although you do not have to swim to get it. When water stays in the ear, it washes away the waterproof layer of earwax in the **ear canal**. The ear canal then stays wet, instead of drying out. **Bacteria** like to grow in damp areas like this. They cause an infection that makes your ear hurt when you touch it. Doctors can cure this with medicines called antibiotics.

People who get swimmer's ear often have narrow ear canals, which trap water easily. Wearing swim hats or ear plugs can protect their ears.

Middle ear infections

Middle ear infections make your ear hurt, and can cause fever and sickness. Children often get them when they have a cold. When germs get into the middle ear, your ear makes pus (a kind of fluid) to attack the germs. If you have a cold, the tube that usually takes fluids away from your ear – called the Eustachian tube – may be blocked with mucus (snot). This makes your ears hurt. If you get ear pain, always have it checked by a doctor.

To avoid middle ear infections, you need to stop catching colds. Always wash your hands before eating, to get rid of germs that could get into your mouth.

WHAT IS GLUE EAR?

Glue ear happens when a sticky fluid (the 'glue') blocks up the middle ear, making it hard to hear. To help, doctors can fit a tiny tube into the **eardrum** to take away the fluid.

15

DO I NEED TO CLEAN MY EYES?

Just like your ears, your eyes are delicate **organs** that should never be prodded or poked. You should wash the outside of your eyes, but your eyes have their own special system for keeping the insides clean – tears.

How should I clean my eyes?

You should wash around your eyes twice a day, in the morning and the evening, when you wash your face. Use a clean flannel and warm water, and dry your face with a clean towel. Dirty flannels and towels can cause and spread **infections**. When you wake up, you may have a sticky or crusty substance in your eye. People call this 'sleep'. It is made up of tears with a little sweat and oil.

Your eyelids, eyebrows and eyelashes catch sweat and other bits of dirt before they get into your eyes. Help them keep your eyes clean by avoiding dusty places.

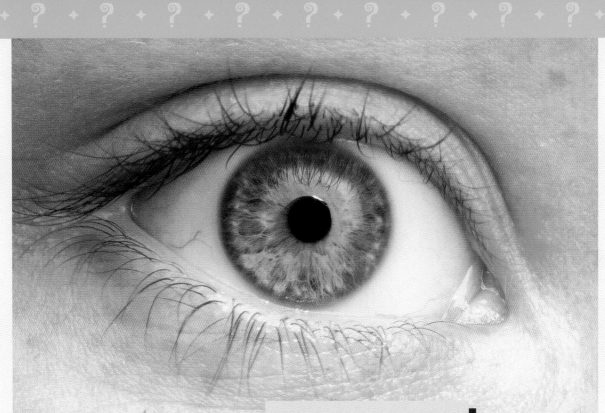

What are tears?

Tears are drops of salty liquid that come from **glands** in your upper eyelid. Every time you blink, a tiny amount of tear fluid comes out of the glands and washes over the eyeball. This tear fluid washes any dust or dirt out of the eye. It also contains a natural disinfectant that kills **germs**, and it stops your eye from drying out.

When tear fluid has washed over the eye, it leaves your eye through a tiny hole called the tear duct.

WHAT IF I GET SOMETHING IN MY EYES?

If you do get something, such as sand or a fly, in your eyes, do not rub them, because this can hurt them. Your eyes will make extra tear fluid to wash them. If there is too much tear fluid to drain out of the tear duct, some of it flows down your cheeks, taking the dirt with it.

WHY DO MY EYES GET SORE?

Your eyes can feel sore for many reasons. If you have a cold, your eyes can ache and feel heavy. If you knock your eye, or a ball hits it, you may get a black eye. This happens when the delicate skin around the eye is bruised. Sometimes, people have sore eyes because of **infections**, such as sties or conjunctivitis.

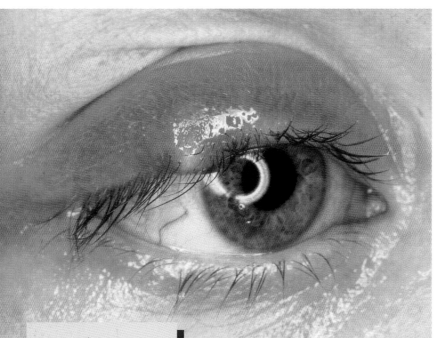

What are sties?

A sty happens when an oil **gland** in your eyelid gets blocked, forming a red, painful lump on your eyelid that looks like a pimple. Sties usually fill with pus and, if they become too big, they can make it hard to open your eye properly. Most sties disappear within a few days, when they burst and the pus drains away.

Most sties are harmless. You only need to see a doctor if you have a sty that does not go away by itself.

What is conjunctivitis?

Conjunctivitis is one of the most common eye problems for children. It makes your eyes red, itchy and swollen, and a sticky liquid collects in the corner. Most children get conjunctivitis from **bacteria** that get into their eye. You can get it when something irritating, such as dirt, gets in your eye. Your doctor will give you eye drops or ointment to put on the eye, to make it better.

Conjunctivitis is easy to pass to other people, or from one eye to another, by touching. You can catch it by touching the hands of a friend who has it. The best way to avoid catching conjunctivitis and many other kinds of infections is to wash your hands often, in warm, soapy water.

You should never use someone else's flannel or towel when you have conjunctivitis, because the sticky liquid can pass on the infection to other people.

WHY SHOULD I WEAR SUNGLASSES?

The **retinas** at the back of your eyes can get burned. Your **pupils** get smaller in bright sunlight, so that not too much light reaches them.

Have you ever wondered why your eyes try to close when you go outside on a bright day? This is to protect themselves from the sunlight. Sunshine can hurt your eyes and the delicate skin around them. To be safe in the sunlight, you should always wear a pair of sunglasses.

How does the sun hurt my eyes?

Sunlight contains ultraviolet, or UV, rays. UV rays are like light, but we cannot see them. They are very strong, and they can cause eye problems, such as cataracts. Cataracts affect the **lens** of the eye. When you are young, your lens is clear. Cataracts are cloudy patches that can form on the lens as you get older. They make the world look cloudy and blurred.

What sorts of sunglasses are best?

Look for sunglasses that offer 100 per cent UV protection. These stop all of the dangerous UV rays in sunlight from hitting your eyes. Choose sunglasses with large frames that wrap around the sides, to protect your eyes from all angles. If you are sporty, choose glasses with shatterproof lenses, which will not break if you fall. Always buy sunglasses from well-known shops, and ask for advice on which fit you best.

WHY WEAR A HAT?

Sun hats help to shade your eyes from the sun, and they protect your ears, face and neck, too. Choose a hat with a brim all the way round, and make sure it is made from tightly woven fabric. Hats with holes in them let sunlight through.

Never look directly at the Sun, even when you are wearing sunglasses. As well as sunglasses, you should always wear a hat in the sun.

21

What other eye protection should I use?

Sunlight is not the only thing that can hurt your eyes. They can also be damaged if bits of wood, metal, chemicals or other things get into them. To prevent this, you should wear protective safety goggles in woodwork and metalwork classes, and when you do some science experiments.

It is also good to wear eye covers for some sports. Swimming goggles not only help you to open your eyes underwater, they also protect your eyes from any **germs** floating in the pool. People sometimes wear shatterproof goggles to stop balls hitting them in the eye in racquet sports, such as squash. Skiers often wear tinted goggles. They protect their eyes from UV rays, and stop bits of ice and snow flying into their eyes as they ski.

Snow can reflect a lot of light. Tinted goggles stop the glare from hurting skiers' eyes.

WHY DO I HAVE TO TAKE COMPUTER BREAKS?

It is easy to lose track of time when you are using the computer, playing with hand-held game toys or watching television. You should take a break from these things every half an hour to rest your eyes, so that you do not strain (weaken) them. If you strain your eyes too much you can damage your eyesight. Take a break, walk around, get a drink or call a friend.

SCREEN SAVERS

Help your eyes by making sure that your computer screen is at least 50 centimetres away from your face. Also make sure that it is at the same level as your eyes. Prop it up with a couple of big books, if you need to.

Look away from the computer screen once in a while, and let your eyes focus on something else. This helps to keep your eyes healthy.

WHY SHOULD I USE A READING LIGHT?

When you read at night, always use a bright lamp that shines light over your book. Don't stay up too late, either. You need plenty of sleep to keep your eyes healthy.

When you read, write or do anything in dim light, the **pupils** in your eyes get bigger (dilate). The eye muscles have to work to dilate the pupils, so that more light gets into your eyes and you can see properly. When you make your eyes work extra hard like this, you make them tired – and you may strain them.

Bedtime lights

When it is time to sleep, turn the lights off. Complete darkness helps your eyes get a good night's rest. It gives them a chance to recover from their hard day's work. If you cannot sleep without a light on, try to use a gentle glow plug, rather than a bright lamp.

WHY SHOULD I HAVE MY EYES AND EARS CHECKED?

It is important for a specialist to check your eyes and ears, because the earlier a problem is detected, the sooner it can be treated. You should visit an optician (eye doctor) for an eye test every two years. Most people only go to the doctor about their ears when they are worried about their hearing.

How do doctors check my ears?

If you are at all worried about your hearing, you should visit the doctor. The doctor will ask about your hearing, and about any illnesses you may have had that might have affected it. They will look into your ear and **eardrum** with a special torch, called an auroscope. If you have an **infection**, the eardrum looks red and swollen.

Using an auroscope, a doctor can also see if you have a blockage in your ear, such as too much earwax, which could be causing problems.

25

Other hearing tests

If the doctor cannot see an obvious reason for your problem, you may need to see an audiologist. An audiologist is a person who carries out special hearing tests. The tests are easy and do not hurt. For example, in one test, you wear earphones and have to press a buzzer each time you hear a noise. If the audiologist finds that you have difficulty hearing, they can fit you with a hearing aid to help you to hear better.

There are many different kinds of hearing aid. This one is worn in the ear, and it makes sounds louder for the wearer.

HOW DO HEARING AIDS WORK?

Hearing aids work by making sounds louder. They pick up sounds through a tiny microphone, and amplify them (make them louder) through an amplifier. The amount of amplification a person needs depends on the kind and level of deafness they have.

What happens during an eye test?

A doctor trained to check eyes is called an optician. They check your eyes inside and out. They look at the outside of your eye to check that your eyes move together properly and look healthy. Then, using a special torch, called an opthalmoscope, they look through the **pupil** of your eye. This lets them check that the inside of the eye is also healthy.

The optician will also ask you to look at an eye chart that is covered in different-sized letters. The optician will cover each of your eyes in turn, and will ask you to read out some of the letters on the chart. From these tests, the optician can tell whether or not you need glasses.

When an optician checks your eyes with an opthalmoscope, they can tell things about your sight, and they can spot other health problems, such as diabetes.

How do glasses help me see?

People wear glasses if the **lenses** in their eyes do not work well. When someone is short-sighted, they can read a book easily, but they cannot see things in the distance. People who are long-sighted can see things in the distance, but they cannot see well close-up. The lenses in glasses correct the problems in your eyes' lenses, so you can see properly.

The lenses in a pair of glasses help you to see. Instead of glasses, some people wear contact lenses on the surface of their eyes.

COLOUR BLINDNESS

Opticians may use special pictures made up of coloured dots to check if you have colour blindness. People who are colour blind cannot tell the difference between some colours. Red and green often look grey to them. This is because some of the **cells** on the **retina** are missing or do not work properly.

EYE AND EAR FACTS

- Our eyes are always the same size from the moment we are born, but our ears never stop growing.

- It is impossible to sneeze with your eyes open.

- A stereo headset playing at full blast (about 110 decibels) could damage your ears in only a half hour!

- We blink more than 10,000 times every day!

- Sounds that are 85 decibels or louder, such as heavy traffic, a noisy restaurant, a screaming child or a lawn mower, can cause hearing damage.

- If you could lay out all the eyelashes that drop out of your eyes in a lifetime, they would stretch over 30 metres.

CARING FOR GLASSES AND HEARING AIDS

It is important to care for glasses and hearing aids, as well as eyes and ears. Follow any instructions the specialist gives you, as well as these tips.

- Clean your glasses daily in warm, soapy water, or with a lens cloth. Always put them away when you are not wearing them.

- Switch your hearing aid off when you are not using it, and store it in its box. Always keep it dry, and clean it with a dry cloth or tissue about once a week.

GLOSSARY

bacteria   tiny living things that can cause disease

cells   smallest building block of living things

cochlea   part of inner ear that looks like a snail shell. It changes sound waves into signals that travel along the auditory (hearing) nerve to the brain.

ear canal   passageway that leads from the outside to the eardrum

eardrum   circular piece of skin (like a drum skin) that separates the outer ear from the middle ear

germs   tiny living things that can cause disease

gland   part of the body that makes substances for use in the body or to be ejected from it

infection   when germs get inside your body and cause disease

inner ear   part of the ear that contains the cochlea and the semi-circular canals

lens   part of the eye that focuses light on to the retina at the back of the eye

middle ear   ear part that includes the ossicles

organ   part of the body that has a particular function, such as the brain, ear or eye

outer ear part of the ear that you can see, and the ear canal, the passageway that leads to the eardrum

pupil hole that lets light into the eye. It looks like a black spot in the middle of the iris.

retina thin layer at the back of the eye

FURTHER READING

Why Do I Get Toothache? And Other Questions About Nerves, Angela Royston (Heinemann Library, 2002)

Why Do My Eyes Itch? And Other Questions About Allergies, Angela Royston (Heinemann Library, 2002)

What Does It Mean To Be Deaf? Louise Spilsbury (Heinemann Library, 2002)

What Does It Mean To Be Blind? Louise Spilsbury (Heinemann Library, 2002)

INDEX

audiologists 26

balance 4, 7, 8
blinking 29
brain 6, 7, 8

cataracts 20
cleaning ears 9, 10
cleaning eyes 16
cochlea 7, 8, 12
conjunctivitis 19

dizziness 8

ear canal 7, 9, 10, 11, 14
ear infections 10, 14-15, 25
eardrum 7, 9, 10, 15, 25
earwax 10-11, 14, 25
eye infections 16, 18-19
eye protection 20-2
eye tests 25, 27

eyelashes 29

germs 10, 11, 14, 15, 17, 22
glasses 28, 29
glue ear 15

hearing aids 26, 29
hearing tests 25-6

lens 6, 20, 28
loud noise 12-13, 29

objects in the ear 5, 9
objects in the eye 5, 17
opticians 25, 27, 28
outer ear 7, 9, 11, 14

pupils 6, 20, 24, 27

retina 6, 20, 28

semi-circular canals 7, 8

senses 4
'sleep' 16
sties 18
sunglasses 20-1
sunhats 21

tears 17
tinnitus 13

UV (ultraviolet) rays 20, 21